A Woman's Guide to Being a Man's Best Friend

A Woman's Guide to Being a Man's Best Friend

by Michael Levin

Andrews and McMeel
A Universal Press Syndicate Company
Kansas City

Library of Congress Catalog Card Number: 96-85618
ISBN 0-8362-2582-1

Design and composition by Steven Brooker of Just Your *Type*.

*This book is
dedicated to
my best friend
Susan Grant*

For all women

Be good to yourself
so you can feel good
about being good
to him

Always tell the truth
even about the
smallest detail

Trust that he will
always tell you the
truth

———◆———

Understand the pressure he feels to be the primary wage earner

Let him know that
his best is good
enough

Let him know it's okay not to always have to be so strong

Don't try to

change him

Understand that in
some ways he'll
always be a little boy
and let it be okay

Don't ever be

demanding

Be his fantasy

Understand his
need to show off
a little

Let him make the
choice when the
choice isn't really
important to you

Baby him when he
doesn't feel well

—◆—

Send him loving
cards or messages
at work

Don't always have
to be right

Encourage him to
fantasize

Compromise easily

Put your arm inside
his as you walk
beside him

Arrange his
pillows so he'll be
comfortable as
he gets ready to
fall asleep

———◆———

Give him a massage

Let him know that
staying home on
Saturday night can
be perfect

Don't shop for
clothes when you
know he is under
financial pressure

Include his favorite
foods in your
shopping list

Be sure he knows
that you are proud
of him

◆

Never embarrass
him

———◆———

Make love to him

Be responsible
for paying the
household bills

Let him pick the
restaurant

Don't compare him
to other men

Listen to him

without interrupting

Never let him see
you looking at
another man

—◆—

Don't smoke or
abuse alcohol and
drugs

Be patient when
he wants to watch
his favorite sports
on T.V.

Listen to him tell
you about his work

———◆———

Make good eye
contact and help
him to do the same

Be patient when
he refuses to get
directions when
he's lost

Light candles in
your bedroom

———◆———

Tell him that he's
the best you've
ever had

◆

Buy him a new
toothbrush every
so often

Live within your
budget

Bring him water

and something for

his headache

———◆———

Balance your
checkbook

———◆———

Wash and fold
his laundry when
you can

Run a bubble bath
for him

Give him a warm
towel from the
dryer when he gets
out of the bath

Be his playmate

Take a shower
with him

Make sure he eats
breakfast

———◆———

Suggest changes
rather than
complaining

Kiss him good-bye
and tell him to be
safe as he leaves
for work

◆

Tell him he's sooo
big and strong

—◆—

Caress him often

Let him pat powder
on you after you
shower

———◆———

Let him rest when
he's tired

Encourage him to
take vitamins and
one aspirin daily

———◆———

Kiss him often on his lips

Thank him for
working so hard

Wear a fragrance

he likes

———◆———

Never talk about
your former
boyfriends

Let him choose the
car he wants to buy

◆

Don't ever imply
that you wish he
earned more money

———◆———

Don't yell at him

Allow him to cry
when he needs
to cry

◆

Put your head on his chest and cuddle with him in the morning

Let him sleep while you're up with your child at night

Share healthy meals together

Don't check up
on him

Don't wear too
much makeup

◆

Prepare the coffee maker so it's ready for him in the morning

Exercise regularly
and encourage him
to do so also

———◆———

Encourage him to go out with his friends

◆

Write all the thank-you notes

Keep the picture albums up to date

Encourage him to
stay in touch with
his family

Tell him you love
the way he looks

———◆———

Accept his need for sexual release

Let him know he
makes you feel good

Encourage him to
reach for his dreams

Maintain a carefully
groomed appearance

Never say anything
which would make
him feel unworthy

Help him to express
his sensitivity

—◆—

Make sure he has
regular physical
checkups

◆

Plan an evening
that's special for
him

———◆———

Understand and be
patient with his
feelings of insecurity
if you earn more
money that he does

———◆———

Help him to feel
lovable

Be patient while
he's learning to be
your best friend

If he's not trying to
be your best friend
forgive yourself
for not wanting to
be his